THIS LAND CALLED AMERICA: **MASSACHUSETTS**

CREATIVE EDUCATION

Published by Creative Education
P.O. Box 227, Mankato, Minnesota 56002
Creative Education is an imprint of The Creative Company
www.thecreativecompany.us

Book and cover design by Blue Design (www.bluedes.com)
Art direction by Rita Marshall
Printed in the United States of America

Photographs by Alamy (Albert Knapp), Corbis (Tony Arruza, Bettmann,
Walter Bibikow, Kevin Fleming, Franz-Marc Frei, Rick Friedman, Jim
Gipe, Kelly-Mooney Photography, Bob Krist, Phil Schermeister, Ted
Spiegel), Getty Images (Altrendo Nature, Aurora, Margaret Bourke-
White//Time Life Pictures, Kean Collection, David Lyons, Michael
Melford, John Nordell//The Christian Science Monitor, Stock Montage,
Time Life Pictures/Mansell/Time Life Pictures, Time Life Pictures/US
Army Signal Corps/Time Life Pictures)

Library of Congress Cataloging-in-Publication Data
Wimmer, Teresa.
Massachusetts / by Teresa Wimmer.
p. cm. — (This land called America)
Includes bibliographical references and index.
ISBN 978-1-58341-646-4
1. Massachusetts—Juvenile literature. I. Title. II. Series.
F64.3.W56 2008
974.4—dc22   2007015014

First Edition
9 8 7 6 5 4 3 2 1

This Land Called America

MASSACHUSETTS

Teresa Wimmer

Massachusetts

TERESA WIMMER

On a warm day at a dock in Hyannis, Massachusetts, tourists wait to board a ferry. From where they are standing, they can see fishermen in their boats hoisting up nets filled with clams and lobsters. As the ferry crosses Nantucket Sound, everyone breathes deeply of the salty sea air and dreams of eating delicious fresh seafood. Once the ferry docks on Martha's Vineyard, the group scrambles onto shore, eager to explore the island's scenic towns and sandy dunes. Children race ahead to gather seashells and look out over the glistening water at some of the natural wonders Massachusetts has to offer.

YEAR

1602   Englishman Bartholomew Gosnold becomes the first European to land in Massachusetts.

EVENT

The Cradle of America

Thousands of years ago, the land of Massachusetts was a wilderness. Many American Indian tribes made its forests their home. A tribe called the Massachusetts camped along the upper eastern coast of the state. Their name meant "near the great hill."

Many of the Indians lived in dome-shaped huts called wigwams. They built the wigwams out of bark, grass, and tree branches. The Indians fished, hunted deer and wild turkeys, and grew crops such as corn, beans, and pumpkins. Some tribes near the coast even hunted whales or trolled for clams.

In 1620, a group of people now called the Pilgrims left their homes in England. They sailed across the Atlantic Ocean on a ship called the *Mayflower*. They landed in Massachusetts and named their new settlement Plymouth. When they landed, the Indians were friendly and offered them gifts.

The Pilgrims (above) were thankful to have reached America safely after 66 days on the rough Atlantic Ocean aboard the Mayflower (opposite).

YEAR
1635   Boston Latin, the first high school in the American colonies, is founded.
EVENT

In 1628, another group of English people sailed for Massachusetts. The Puritans landed in 1629 and founded the Massachusetts Bay Colony near Salem. They lived a strict life. They did not dance or play instruments. They did not go to any plays, either. They wanted to focus their lives on God and believed that having fun was a distraction.

The Puritans were very superstitious. When two girls in Salem began to have mysterious fits in 1692, Puritan leaders blamed witches for casting spells on them. Soon, a "witch hunt" erupted in the town. In the end, 150 women were jailed or killed before the town could put an end to the trials.

Over time, more people from Europe came to Massachusetts. In cities along the coast, shipbuilding became a big business. Ships were provided to merchants. Then merchants were able to sell fish, corn, salt, and lumber to other countries across the ocean.

In the 1700s, England placed a tax on colonists' paper goods and tea. The colonists did not have a voice in the British government and did not want to pay their taxes. Some colonists were so angry with the British that they dressed up like Indians and dumped 342 chests of British tea into Boston Harbor, an event known as the Boston Tea Party.

The Boston Tea Party (opposite) occurred on December 16, 1773, and involved about 60 men.

YEAR
1690
EVENT
America's first newspaper, *Publick Occurrences Both Forreign and Domestick*, is published in Boston.

- *9* -

Textile mills such as those owned by the American Woolen Co. were found throughout Massachusetts.

Soon, England sent soldiers to Massachusetts to keep order. One night in 1775, British soldiers were spotted marching toward the towns of Lexington and Concord. A Massachusetts man named Paul Revere rode his horse from Boston through the night to warn the colonists. The next morning, the British fought the colonists in the first battle of the Revolutionary War. After the war ended, the colonies became the United States, with Massachusetts being admitted as the sixth state in 1788.

In the 1800s, many people from Poland, Russia, Italy, and Ireland came to live in growing cities such as Boston and Lowell. Chinese people came to build railroads. Along Massachusetts's riverbanks, mills sprang up. The mills turned cotton into cloth and made furniture, ships, and leather goods.

Mill workers worked long hours at dangerous jobs for low pay. Some of them went on strike to achieve better working conditions. Educators also thought children in the state should receive a better education. They worked to reform Massachusetts's schools. By the early 1900s, other public schools in the U.S. followed Massachusetts's example.

YEAR

1716 Boston Light, the oldest lighthouse in the country, opens in Boston Harbor.

EVENT

The Bay State

MASSACHUSETTS IS A SMALL STATE, BUT IT HAS MANY DIFFERENT TYPES OF LANDSCAPES. MORE THAN HALF OF THE STATE IS COVERED BY FORESTS. ITS SHORELINES ARE TIPPED WITH SAND BLOWN INTO HILLS CALLED DUNES, AND ROLLING FIELDS AND SNOWCAPPED MOUNTAINS LIE NEARBY.

On the northern side, Vermont and New Hampshire border Massachusetts. Rhode Island and Connecticut are neighbors to the south, and New York forms its western border. To the east, Massachusetts is rimmed by the beautiful bays of the Atlantic Ocean. That is why it is called "The Bay State."

The biggest bay is Cape Cod Bay, named for the huge schools of codfish that once swarmed in its waters. Cod still live there, along with other fish, clams, oysters, and lobsters. Along the shore, tall grasses sprout through rocky, sandy dunes. The soft, wet, low-lying lands called marshes along the shore are home to gulls, ducks, and other shorebirds.

North of Cape Cod Bay lies Massachusetts Bay. Massachusetts's capital city, Boston, was built along this bay. More than 30 small islands, which were once used as summer fishing camps by Indians, can be found in the bay. Later, colonists farmed on them, and a few islands became places where rich people built summer homes.

In the southeastern corner of the state, the land slopes downward and becomes wet and marshy. The soggy land is good for growing cranberries. Cranberry bogs make the land look like a red sea. Nearby and just off the coast lie the islands of Martha's Vineyard and Nantucket. Thousands of grapevines grow on Martha's Vineyard.

On Cape Cod (above), the hook-shaped part of the state, much of the flat, marshy land bordering the bay is broken up by water (opposite).

YEAR
1770   English soldiers kill five colonists in a conflict known as the Boston Massacre.
EVENT

The Connecticut River is Massachusetts's longest river. It courses through the middle of the state and is surrounded by rolling hills and valleys, which are dotted with violets and other wildflowers each spring. The river makes the soil rich, and it gives the dirt a reddish-brown color. Apple orchards make the air smell crisp and fruity. Farmers grow other fruits, corn, and beans in the area. They also raise animals such as cattle.

Other important rivers are the Merrimack, Mystic, and Charles. The Charles River runs through the city of Boston. White-tailed deer and beavers can be found along Massachusetts's rivers—even in the cities. Near the town of Webster in the middle of the state is a lake with the longest

The Connecticut River (above) serves an important purpose throughout New England, including enriching farmland used to grow crops (opposite).

1814 Francis Cabot Lowell opens a textile mill in Waltham, launching the textile industry in the U.S.

*Boston's Charles
River is the setting for
recreational activities
such as sailing, rowing,
and sculling.*

Charles River

name in the world: Lake Chargoggagoggmanchaugagogg-
chaubunagungmaug. Locals just call it "Lake Webster."

West of the Connecticut River, the land becomes increas-
ingly hilly. The Berkshire Hills form a mountain range of green
valleys and high peaks. The cool mountain streams are filled
with salmon and trout. Mount Greylock—the state's highest
point at 3,491 feet (1,064 m)—is in the Berkshires. Ash, maple,
oak, and birch trees fill the forests. In the fall, their leaves turn
bright shades of red, orange, and gold.

People in Massachusetts never know what the weather
will bring. In the summer, the days are usually hot and humid.
But breezes from the Atlantic Ocean cool the cities along the
shore. Summer days can be rainy, stormy, or sunny. Winters
are cold with lots of snow. Sometimes, a big winter storm
called a nor'easter travels up Massachusetts's east coast. It
dumps a lot of snow on the state. In 1978, a nor'easter dropped
three feet (.9 m) of snow in 36 hours.

*Mount Greylock (visible
in the background above)
has been known by that
name since the 1830s.*

YEAR
1876 Alexander Graham Bell invents the telephone in Boston.
EVENT

Living in Massachusetts

In Massachusetts, more than six million people live in a small space. That makes the state crowded. Half of the population lives in or around Boston. The city and the state have a long history of welcoming people within their borders.

In the 1840s, thousands of Irish men and women came to Massachusetts. They left their homes in Ireland because they did not have enough food there. Many people were dying of hunger. In Massachusetts, they found jobs and food.

The children of many Irish immigrants grew up to become police officers, judges, and politicians in Massachusetts. The 35th president of the U.S., John Fitzgerald Kennedy, came from a long line of Irish politicians. He was born in Brookline in 1917. In 1963, he was assassinated while riding in a car in Dallas, Texas.

After the Irish, many other immigrants moved to Massachusetts. They came from countries such as Canada, Germany, Italy, and Poland. They came to work in the lumber, paper, textile, and leather mills. Some opened shops and restaurants. Others farmed or grew fruit.

A planter and missionary named John Chapman grew up around apple orchards in Leominster County, Massachusetts,

Boston's Faneuil Hall Marketplace (opposite) and festive parades (above) offer opportunities for people to gather in the city.

Johnny Appleseed visited the homes of many pioneer families on his journey west.

in the 1770s. As an adult in the early 1800s, he preached the message of Christianity and distributed apple seedlings to farmers in Ohio, Illinois, and Indiana. He became known as Johnny Appleseed.

Today, most people in Massachusetts are white. African Americans make up the next largest group. A few descendants of American Indians still live in the state, making their homes mainly on Cape Cod and Martha's Vineyard. Hispanics are the third-largest group in the state. The fastest growing populations are Southeast Asian and Caribbean Americans.

People today work in many different jobs in Massachusetts. Some work in factories that make parts for computers and other machines, or places that produce books and maga-

YEAR
1897   America's oldest and most famous footrace, the Boston Marathon, is first run.
EVENT

1914   The Cape Cod Canal, a narrow waterway between Cape Cod and mainland Massachusetts, opens.

zines. Other people work in hotels, hospitals, law firms, and schools. Harvard University, in Cambridge, is the country's oldest college. More than 20 of the U.S.'s most highly regarded colleges and universities are in the Boston area.

Before her work as a Civil War nurse, Clara Barton founded a successful free school in 1852.

Mining and fishing are important to the state as well. People mine for hard rocks such as marble and granite. The Washington Monument in Washington, D.C., is made from Massachusetts marble. Fishermen still make their living from the bays. They catch lobsters, clams, oysters, and many kinds of fish.

Good health has always been important to people in Massachusetts. The country's first woman allowed onto a battlefield, Clara Barton, was born in 1821 in North Oxford. During the Civil War of the 1860s, she volunteered to lead a group of nurses in caring for wounded soldiers. Barton was called the "Angel of the Battlefield." In 1881, she started the American Red Cross. This organization has helped care for millions of people worldwide since then.

YEAR

1919 | A huge molasses tank bursts in Boston, and 21 people drown in the sticky substance.

EVENT

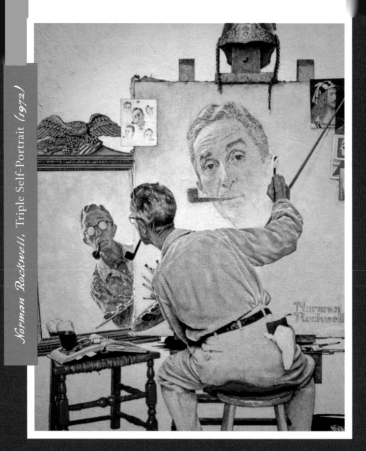

Massachusetts can claim many important writers and poets, including Louisa May Alcott. Alcott grew up in Boston and Concord in the mid-1800s. As a child, she loved to write stories that she and her sisters acted out. When she was 35, she wrote a book called *Little Women*. Based on her life, it is the story of four sisters growing up in New England. The book made Alcott famous and is considered an American classic.

American illustrator Norman Rockwell (above) lived on the opposite end of the state from Louisa May Alcott (opposite) and died almost a century later.

1938 A hurricane known as the "Long Island Express" kills hundreds and floods coastal cities.

Food, Festivals, and Fun

WHEN PEOPLE VISIT ANY PART OF MASSACHUSETTS, THEY FIND THERE IS A LOT TO SEE AND DO. IN THE SUMMER, PEOPLE ENJOY HIKING AND BIKING IN THE BERKSHIRES. THEY ALSO CANOE AND FISH IN RIVERS FILLED WITH TROUT AND BASS. IN WINTER, SKIERS SWISH DOWN THE SNOWY SLOPES.

Between the cities of Greenfield and Williamstown, people can drive along the Mohawk Trail. The trail was made by Indians 500 years ago. Today, people can stop along the trail to see spots where American Indian battles once happened.

South of Worcester, in the central part of the state, people can visit Old Sturbridge Village to see what colonial life was like. They can walk through a working farm, school, mill, bank, and home. In Springfield, sports fans can visit the Basketball Hall of Fame. The game of basketball was invented there by James Naismith in 1891. The Hall of Fame tells visitors about the greatest basketball players ever.

Along the coast at Cape Ann, daily whale-watching boats go out to sea. Lucky visitors might catch a glimpse of these beautiful animals. People can also enjoy eating fresh seafood at one of the many restaurants near the bays.

It is worth traveling to Massachusetts just to visit Boston. The country's oldest park, Boston Common, is near the center of town. The Freedom Trail starts there, too. The Trail takes visitors past 16 places that were important in the story of the American Revolution, such as Paul Revere's house and the USS *Constitution*.

Just off the coast of Boston is the Charlestown Navy Yard. It keeps the USS *Constitution*—the country's first warship—in its dock. The ship is nicknamed "Old Ironsides" because even cannonballs could not sink it. Today, the ship serves as

In the capital city of Boston, people can see many sites, including Boston Common (opposite), and taste the fresh seafood (above).

In 2007, Boston used 20,000 pounds (9 t) of explosives to put on a spectacular fireworks display on July 4.

a museum and as part of Boston Harbor's spectacular Fourth of July celebration.

The New England Aquarium gives people close-up views of underwater life. It has a giant ocean tank that is four stories high! Visitors feel as though they could almost touch the sharks, giant sea turtles, and tropical fish. The sea lions at the aquarium also put on a good show.

No visit to Boston would be complete without riding the subway. It is the oldest subway system in the country. The train is part of a transit system that runs both underground and on tracks above crowded streets. Today, the transit line travels to 175 cities and towns in Massachusetts.

People in Massachusetts love to celebrate holidays. The St. Patrick's Day parade in Boston is one of the world's largest. Each winter, Boston holds a First Night celebration on New Year's Eve that features ice sculptures and fireworks. In the

YEAR
1974 Boston's public schools are ordered to desegregate. Students of different races now attend all the same schools.
EVENT

At the New England
Aquarium, people can
see such sea creatures
as jellyfish (below),
penguins, and seals.

Jane Swift becomes the first woman to serve as governor of Massachusetts.

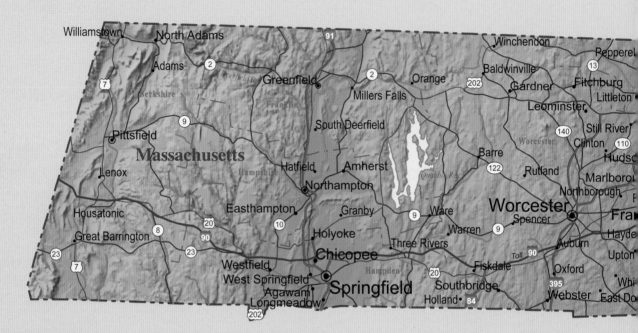

fall, the town of Plymouth recreates the first Thanksgiving
that was celebrated by the Pilgrims and American Indians.
Summer on Nantucket Island features the Sandcastle Contest.
Contestants of every age compete to build the biggest and
best castles.

Teams from nearly every professional sport are at home
in Boston, from hockey's Bruins to basketball's Celtics. The
Patriots play football and the Revolution play soccer in Gillette
Stadium. Each summer, baseball fans can cheer for the Red
Sox at Fenway Park. With so much to see, do, and cheer about
in Massachusetts, visitors just might be tempted to stay.

QUICK FACTS

Population: 6,398,743

Largest city: Boston (pop. 581,616)

Capital: Boston

Entered the union: February 6, 1788

Nickname: Bay State

State flower: mayflower

State bird: chickadee

Size: 10,555 sq mi (27,337 sq km)—44th-biggest in U.S.

Major industries: manufacturing, farming, fishing, education, tourism

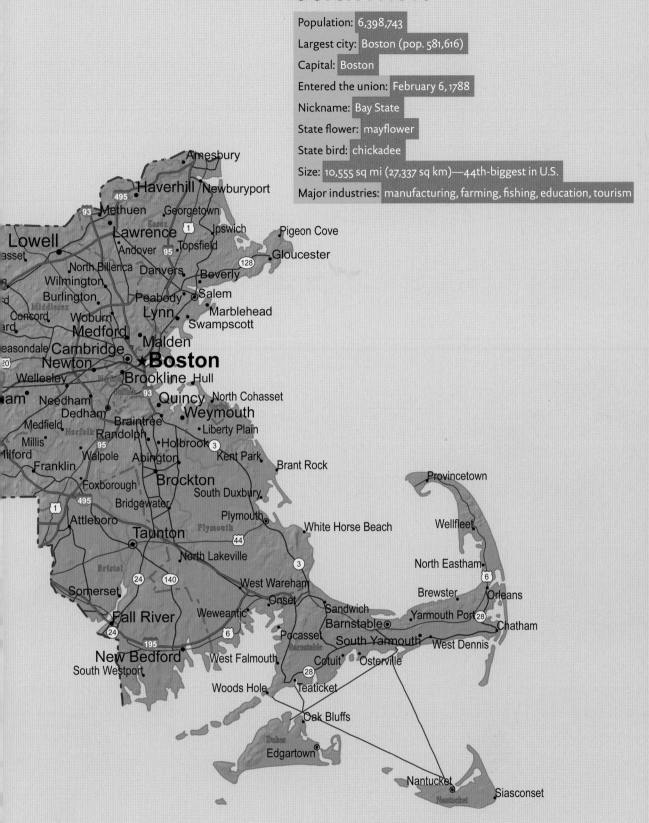

Amesbury

Haverhill • Newburyport

93 Methuen • Georgetown

Lowell

asset

Lawrence • Ipswich • Pigeon Cove

Andover 95 • Topsfield

North Billerica • Danvers • Gloucester 128

Wilmington • Beverly

Burlington • Peabody • Salem

Concord • Woburn • Lynn • Marblehead

Medford • Swampscott

easondale Cambridge • Malden

Newton ★Boston

Wellesley Brookline • Hull

am 93 Quincy • North Cohasset

Needham Weymouth

Dedham Braintree • Liberty Plain

Medfield Randolph • Holbrook 3

Millis 95 Abington • Kent Park

Milford Walpole Brockton • Brant Rock

Franklin

Foxborough • South Duxbury

495 Bridgewater • Plymouth

Attleboro • White Horse Beach

Taunton 44

North Lakeville

Somerset 24 140 West Wareham

Fall River Weweantic • Onset

24 195 6 Pocasset

New Bedford • West Falmouth • Cotuit

South Westport

Woods Hole 28 • Teaticket

Provincetown

Wellfleet

North Eastham 6

Brewster • Orleans

Yarmouth Port 28 • Chatham

Sandwich

Barnstable

South Yarmouth • West Dennis

Osterville

Oak Bluffs

Edgartown

Nantucket

Siasconset

YEAR

2004 Massachusetts senator John Kerry is defeated by George W. Bush in the presidential election.

EVENT

- 31 -

BIBLIOGRAPHY

Harris, Patricia, and David Lyon. *Art of the State: Massachusetts*. New York: Harry N. Abrams, 1999.

Harris, Patricia, et al. *Massachusetts*. New York: Compass American Guides, 2003.

Leotta, Joan. *Massachusetts*. New York: Children's Press, 2001.

LeVert, Suzanne. *Massachusetts*. New York: Benchmark Books, 2000.

Louisa May Alcott Memorial Association. "Louisa May Alcott." Orchard House—Home of the Alcotts. http://www.louisamayalcott.org/louisamaytext.html.

Massachusetts Office of Travel & Tourism. "Massachusetts." http://www.massvacation.com/jsp/index.jsp.

INDEX